Spider Silk

A COLLECTION OF POETRY

Danah Slade

Copyright © 2024 by Danah Slade

All rights reserved. No part of this book may be reproduced or transmitted in any form or by any means, electronic or mechanical, including photocopy, recording, or any information storage and retrieval system, without permission in writing from the publisher.

No part of this work may be performed without written consent of publisher.

All characters, businesses, organisations, places and events are either the product of the author's imagination and used fictitiously. Any resemblance to events or locales is entirely co-incidental. Any poems addressed to actual persons will not be named, protected by the anonymity of initials.

ISBN 978-1-76350-051-8

Cover Art by Danah Slade

Obsidian Moth Publishing

For all enquiries email: slade.enquiries@gmail.com

Other books by this Author

2024 – No Promises by Danah Slade
2025 – Vertebrae Letters by Danah Slade

Preface

In Australia, *Beyond Blue* reports the LGBTQIA+ community has the highest rates of suicide and suicide attempts. *'Spider Silk'* confronts the systemic oppression that contributes to these heart-wrenching statistics, touching specifically on repression, being a common state queer people find themselves in.

In the least accepting parts of the world, leading a queer lifestyle is a criminal offense, even punishable by death. In more tolerant societies, individuals still feel compelled to hide non-traditional relationships to protect themselves and partners. This active burial of oneself and beliefs, is a form of death too. I wrote this book to flip this narrative, to challenge the hatred that has cost so many LGBTQIA+ lives. My intention was to illustrate the enduring presence of queer voices beyond death.

The way love and death are intrinsically connected, especially in queer relationships, is intriguing to me. These are large, seemly contrasting themes, however, poets find themselves drawn to them time and time again. What eludes logical understanding insists on being unpacked emotionally. Here, we find ample room for personal interpretation and creativity.

Writing this book was an inner exploration throughout the years of 2020-2022. I blended real-life events with fiction, as a vessel to explore my farsighted desires and fears. I often adopted a first-person perspective for clarity, especially when gender pronouns may cause confusion between unnamed characters. Historical references were interwoven to tackle stereotypes and stigmas rooted in the past. The awareness given to laws against homosexuality, witches amongst other villainised feminine icons resulted in a cynical romanticist style. It was my attempt at a reclamation or a rewrite, without the erasure.

The notion of queer relationships being 'unnatural' is a result of heteronormativity. *'Spider Silk'* is since laced with nature imagery, serving as an overarching metaphor enforcing queerness as natural. Furthermore, contrasting and relieving the heavy topics within the pages.

Upon beginning this collection, my question was; what is this veracity within us that breaks through generations of cultural conditioning to bring us face-to-face with ourselves? I grew up in a religious setting and to this day, I'm still questioning my subconscious programming. Peeling back layers of shame around my sexuality and gender.

If *'Spider Silk'* doesn't bring you consolation like it did for me, I hope it is a fruitful confrontation.

Table of Contents

SHE'S THE SKELETON IN MY CLOSET	11
SPIRALLED SHELL	12
THE NIGHTFLOWER THIEF	13
TRAVELLER	14
GRAVEYARD	15
ACCIDENTAL EFFIGIES	16
(AFTER)PARTY	17
CRIME SCENE	18
BLACKLIGHT AND LUMINOL	21
BLOOD MAGICK	22
SELF-DOUBT DOESN'T DISCRIMINATE	23
SKY-CLAD DANCING	24
THE SLOWEST ACCIDENT	25
INVOCATION	26
A SÉANCE OF SORTS	27
OBSIDIAN MIRROR	28
THE VOTE	29
LOVE AND OTHER CLICHÉS	30
POACHER PRIEST	31
EYE OF HER STORM	32
STRAIGHT, MOTHER	33
PERFUME	34
PORTALS	35
SPIDER SILK	36

SPIDER SILK II	37
NYCTINASTY	38
THE SEASONS	39
SABOTEUR	40
FIRST KISS	41
RIPEN AGAINST SHADOWS	42
CRESCENDO	43
HER – I – SEA	44
SIREN AND SORCERESS	45
SAVAGEFACTION	46
OUR ELEMENT	47
SHARK	48
9 KISSES OF MEDUSA	49
SHARK II	51
ECLIPSED	52
TO WISH FOR YOU	53
SEAMLESS INCISIONS	55
WAR PAINT	56
DEAR B,	57
HONEY	59
THE BEAST	60
WHY DO YOU GO TO A MAN?	61
CRYPTOLOGIST	62
NEVER YOU	63
IN MEMORY OF MARIE	65
MY BLOOD	67
DATING APPS AND COUNTRY TOWNS	68

IF IT'S PHYSICAL	69
RUM AND VANILLA EXTRACT	70
ELSA	73
BLOODY MARY	74
ON-STAGE CHEMISTRY	75
CRYSTAL SHOP DATE	76
PHANTOM	77
TWO LIFE PATHS	78
CRIMES YOU WANT ME TO COMMIT	79
THE WHOLE DAMN ARSENAL	80
MY CRYPT/TONIGHT	81
ASSASSIN	82
OBSERVATIONS OF FLORISTRY STUDENT	84
OBSERVATIONS OF FLORISTRY STUDENT	85
LAST WORDS	86
THE MORGUE	87
CATACOMBS	88
IMMORTALITY	89
AFTERLIFE	90
SHE TO HER	91
FRACTURAL FEMME FATALE LYRICS	92
FUTURE ME THIS	94
HEARTH	97

She's the Skeleton in My Closet

Most people fight to keep their love alive,
I labour differently; continuously *nailing* mine in an upright coffin.
I must: preserve her cheeks pale, heart cold and eyes unblinking.
She's the skeleton in my closet.

Foreboding of a confession, forbidden obsession,
every time her name brushes past my lips.
A real kiss might be less obvious.

Secrecy threatens to lessen.
Do I shiver – fearful or invigorated?
It's as if she, I have killed,
'*Come out* with it!', guilt weighs heavy. That,
with Pride, 'Look how I've made her mine'.

They must never discover the vivacity in her bones;
for that is to know my own heart
that beats against them, along with my butterflies
trapped within.

Should they observe how she almost blushes or blinks,
more gaze than glazed-over when she looks at me –
should they know of the *life* I inspire within her;
I would faster claim the title of Murderess.
Taking her out, becomes just that;
a narrative easier for them to digest.

They would faster *tie the knot*, eternal
in our stomachs than our hands.

My sexuality is not, but is limited to:
an outfit change,
reasonable only to *hook-up* in the closet.

Spiralled Shell

I have detached myself
from my care for you
in identity, in emotion, in denial
and if that's what it takes to survive
I will float so far away
your heaven will have no choice but to take me.

                                        Until you find: I'm no longer
                                             in the spiralled shell
                                                 you made of me,
                                                     and too, vacate.

Until, slowly,
the letters of my own name
form a mantra
I can return home to.

The Nightflower Thief
P.F.

The beautiful Nightflower Thief,

has a compulsion to pick every flower she comes across
and place them on the dashboard
of her car.

At the O'Connell bakery she targets the Jasmine
like she's shoplifting.
Stubbornly pulling it off the bush
and stuffing it in her pocket.

At my house she takes the Abelia,
lifting it to her nose;
a wholesome drug.

On Ninth Avenue
– a neighbourhood exploding in Christmas lights –
we stop for 10 minutes as she fixates on a rose.
Waiting for foot-traffic to lighten
before she darts her hand through the picket fence.

Her name in Sanskrit refers to the full moon
but she's citrus of the sun;
bright, invigorating and
tipping tabasco over absolutely everything,
including her drinks.

A montage of red lipstick;
clothing doused in more colour and patterns
than I thought any material could possibly hold.

Life follows her.

I wonder when she will lift me from her pocket...
Notice, I've always been medicinal –
thistles, weeds;
not the type to distinguish an
arrangement.

Traveller

Over 2 million miles away,
there's a woman wearing my hair tie.

An odd woodland green,
which survived high school.
The only one I hadn't lost
since moving cities
and the closest to hand
the day before
she rolled out of my bed
onto an aircraft.

Today, I found the one she left behind,
looped it through my sooty mane.
An elucidation;
elastics are the rings
wedding a profusion of dynamics.

A commonality misplaced
becomes rarity.

I gaze out the window of my bus,
the sweat of continents
I've never visited, entwined in my hair.

These roads – too – are strands,

praise each rotation
I am closer to lost or entangled.

Graveyard

Unravel me, paint me anew,
find me in brushstrokes.
Folds. Curves. Shadows.

Then you'll know,
before you saw all,
before you touched all –
I was never complete.
Whole, but not in colour.

The way a poem stands
with the finest structure,
but begs to be
dissected again,
vertebrae-letters, restrung.

My body; just a graveyard
for my bones
before you came along.

Tip the inkwell of my eyes;
make all of me
dilate.

Accidental Effigies

I

Under moonlight, your body the colour of Icelandic sands,
ash of volcanic eruptions that linger on from last
daybreak; where then, your skin was lit with magma undertones –
burning, engulfing me, stopping me dead
like a victim of Pompeii forever reaching
for spirit to fill this cast again.

II

We made ourselves into accidental effigies
in this town. They hold signs like 'love isn't love *if...*'
use us as anti-mascots
like we weren't once alive.

They climb inside me,
redirect my outstretched arm

until I appears, I no longer reach for you.

(After)Party

Veiled then
aisles drawn upon us
and when they send us away
we let them.
The honeymoon
customarily, a place of heat.
Cremains upon the air,
our own *after* party
c

        o   n

                         f   e

                                        tti.

Crime Scene

I dreamt of a technology
which scanned the walls of crime scenes.

Graphed temperature so precisely;
it could reshape the coldness of a shadow

                                            draped across a wall
            from hours prior.

Every movement; a frame
replaying blurred silhouettes
of a life and its end.

If we are ever considered a crime scene,
you'd doubtlessly be my kill.*Switch*.

I could recognise you in the haziest form
But would they ever   catch you?

Like I promised, to always be there to
                                      catch you?

*Maybe they'd outline where you'd been
in chalk too..*

The living haunt the dead;
a murder
of camera shutters like crow's   wings.

Our story not *carved* into a tree trunk,
or *locked* on a bridge but
chalk that washes away with the rain.

If we are ever considered a crime scene,
help them link the red string between us.

Tell them the Chinese legend; lines of fate
like infrared lasers – invisible to the human eye.

Imagine if they could suddenly see their own soul ties;
every type of lover and lesson indistinguishable;
taking aim *before* reason.

If they could see how it goes both ways;
follow the lines from their own pinkie triggers.
Just…
       be just.

Would they then, see us as more than that surface?
Would they then, call our crime scene what it was?
Call it, law evasion not home invasion.
Call it, the gentlest body-snatching.

If we are ever considered a crime scene,
promise we'll leave evidence everywhere.
Promise, we'll make an advent calendar
of those little yellow markers;
numbers
inhabiting every. bit. of. space;

our memories exhibited

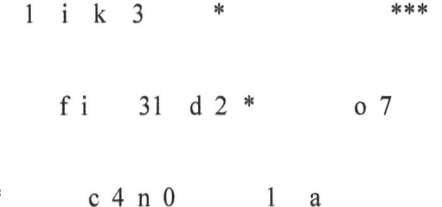

When they canvas(s) the area,
let it be a reminder;
we were art.

Blacklight and Luminol

I am not blue
like porcelain plates,
the surface of sea or lake,
blood drained from a face.

I am Nightmare Planet blue,
they'll caution you;
my lachrymose is molten
a glass storm –
raining parallel
They'll caution you   but overlook
my devotion   of it all;
sacrificial atmosphere –
How I burn away, just to be closer.

I am Blue Dragon blue;
venom not my own
but a transference amplified.
Meet me at my antitheses.
A dance where we may both lead
and follow
under the siphonophore
of our hunger.

I am venous marbling blue,
a horror of humanity – I am told.
But if our blood is all that remains,
let it speak to our fluorescence.
Blacklight and luminol divulging our (after)glow;

the most valid blue-light
to keep them up at night.

Blood Magick

It's no lie,
she has magick that could segregate seas.
A simple wave of her hand above my flesh
has my tides surging to that part.
Tell me how this isn't some form of witchcraft.

Self-Doubt Doesn't Discriminate
On Internalised-Homophobia

There are still legal exorcisms in this country, forced upon those who are gay. Degrees extinguished... Faster than alarms can sound, in church-run universities. The past isn't a ghost, it's still creating history. Trauma; an accent we've adopted into our voices and cannot separate.

We set the bar so low, it was treated like a tripwire.

Maybe it's them I should blame. Maybe it's me, listening until it was engrained. Maybe I don't know the definition of love because it doesn't make me want to shout from rooftops; doesn't loud and proud go hand-in-hand? Aren't I supposed to like rainbows not storms? I talk to myself like a conversion therapist more often than not. Fighting against what I know is right while giving the opposing side more reasons to demonise.

The fragile and hostile are the easiest to brainwash, I'm scared they'll get at me with their cloths. Hesitation *must* mean lies; and spite is surely armouring something broken inside. What a convenient way to keep us silent, hiding, undefined and undefiant.

Tell me, when did self-doubt become a plausible excuse to come at our youth from both sides? Bible Bashers, Gay Gate Keepers. *You're right, we are confused...* by this system of oppression and abuse.

Tell me, haven't all great artists wanted to scribble over their masterpieces
because they forget their worth some days?

Why must I question if I have enough pride to walk those marches?
Why must I rejoice in each straight person who tolerates me?
Why must I feel the urge to justify loving a girl?

See, I am also a girl
and it's taken enough to accept myself.

Sky-Clad Dancing

Sky-clad; waist spinning,
head rolling and hair flicking in spirals.
Hips dipping forward
as she tiptoes in-time to bass strums.
Calves taut before she drops, slinky not of wire
but bending knees and rippling tummy;
a thousand rings of fire.

I write these lines in those,
her crev*erses;*
or rather, embolden them – a line upon a line.

My hands then shave down shoulders
'til threaded with hers, I step-step to embrace her from behind.
Chest imprints her back like engraving a tablet.
'Remember these sweat-dripped, bonfire-lit dusks.
Recover the illustrations I've left of us,
on us.'

Our cheeks knock together,
seeping comatose and chamomile.
Crackling, smoking,
laughing and kissing like foolish

fireworks;   ^
every explosion a splendid shatter then rain.   ^   ^   ^
I've never known one to harness all that   < b r e a k s > them
to be so loud, menacing and magnificent   v   v   v
– at once.   v

Will you answer the rumble, deep and beckoning?
Amend the tendrils of smoke,
jump with me, this Beltane, and leave the world
shaking harder than before
when our feet speak to the ground
like a needle over a record.

The Slowest Accident

N. K.

We didn't kiss at Club Curious,
as she leaned into me on the dance floor.

We didn't kiss at 4am in the city gardens
having run out of words
shivering but reluctant to move.

We didn't kiss wrapped up in bed
nor on the hike, finding ourselves under the native mistletoe.

We kissed like it was an accident.

The slowest accident anyone could ever prevent.
Millimetres closer at a time.

Fifteen minutes of fingers persuading necks they're the extension
of the shoulder, of the arm, of the hand, of fingers;
of themselves,
of friendly affection.

Noses touching softly as fairy floss,
then tilting
to melted sugar.

Her easy nails on my back,
gradually revealing their ravenous.

And when we broke for breath
I mocked, as if I didn't know
mistletoe

is never a coincidence
mid-March.

Invocation

Let's play that game of whispers.
Spell your desires in

                                                stAcCaTo notes,
                                        even curse~ive strokes.

Then, I will try
to recite them back to you.

                                                Whatever it is –

I want to learn you.
This is the only way I will ever play you
so let me do it well;

                                                    show me

on me
first.

A Séance of Sorts

Their bodies are Ouija boards,
                      planchette eyes
                                        – heart shaped –
        slide over each other;
                            delivering every
                    unwritten letter

                                  of their obituaries.

Obsidian Mirror

      No need to correct sins

where choirs   could never sing.

           But by all means,

cast aside   the obsidian mirror,   the tea leaves –

If to endear

           me.

           Seer through my skin;

unravel an omen

       from the undulating   verte-braille within.

The Vote
2017

I was taken at 16
to my friend's church
the morning after her birthday.

The preacher was up-in-arms,
"What is this world coming to?"
"The Devil is testing us"
"…evil if you say YES".

The Gay Marriage Bill was yet to be passed.
I didn't know the importance back then,
just knew how I felt;
discomfort in that room – full
but figured it was only because I was new.

Love and Other Clichés

Honey, wild flower;
you are both the product of my love and the reason for it.

I know it cliché to decorate poems with petals and sunshine
but they're unsurpassed in describing
how you take in every form of light, despite shadows
and grow from it.

I hate that I harbour most of those shadows.
I hate that I must often hide in yours, though I am their creator.

I plead to the waning moon,
'Please don't make me leave her,
don't turn her 'shine' into 'shunned''.
I ask people don't look at
our two wombs and wish us misfortune.
I ask

though, you've already been taken,
withered by the wind,
your remnants spiral sombre past me
so I may hear the sough of your sentiment one last time.

Poacher Priest

You see a lioness; the way she wields her Pride.
It makes you doubt yourself;
forget in whom her biggest predator lies.

Eye of Her Storm

Eye of her storm, apple of   my eye. I take her in. Sin.

    The fruit was never the   matter. She is the fruit.

Neither the harvesting. It was the listening. So, heed my words

    when I say, 'I pick her'. 'Whatever the cost'.

    Everything has a price, all things are a sin

    in someone's eyes. But me,

    her, we   –   our values

    lie in   love not

    rules of

    rust.

Straight, Mother

Straight like a smile.
Straight like every bone in the human body.
Straight.

Straight like the mountainside.
Straight like the moon in every phase.
Straight.

Straight like the nest of a bird.
Straight like the surface of the earth.
Straight.

Straight like a woman's figure
Straight because it's more 'natural'.
Straight.

Yes Mother,
I
I
I
I
I
I
 I
I
am straight.

Perfume

I want it to be her and I,
in the mornings but mostly the nights.
I want to hear a pencil scratching as I type.
See my wardrobe being worn before I open its door.
To smell of perfume without lifting it from my dresser.

Portals

I watch myself
become glaciated within her eyes,
thinking of the way mirrors open portals
when facing each other.
I speculate if that's what's brewing between us now.
Through yet beyond our sight;
miniscule images bouncing back and forth with
every shared gaze.
Is this what it means to see infinity in someone's eyes?

Spider Silk

   Spidery fingertips whisper around your collar –
caressing your tears like they're precious jewels
   and softly lacing a connection between you;

like a shared garment – bulletproof.
An armour, her delicate fibres may form.

   She, fatality technician,
  your gossamer bride amending

     chandelier of dew.

    Captivating even in her transparency.
      Spectacle yet no specimen of the sun,
      a gift of predawn.

Spider Silk II

Light rainfall kindles
    more warmth inside;

        she moves in circles
           but you're the one becoming
           dizzy.

        Somehow, continuing to stridulate
           against her stomach
        long after

                she devours you in her silk.

Nyctinasty

(The circadian movement of plants in response to darkness)

We press flowers at midnight.

After tulips tuck themselves in at nightfall
and ants hurry away before rain,

dripping dark places become our Elysium
to unfurl and cross-pollinate.

I hear the crunch of her hair in my fist,
her fingers feathering over my every rib.

Oh, to write of the stories
only walls cinemise in silhouettes.

The Seasons

Tell me your favourite season…
If it's spring I am fragrant.
If it's summer I am bold.
If it's autumn I am blushing.
If it's winter I am bare.

Saboteur

G.S. 3/6/2022

I warm my hands around my green tea,
lounge back in an antique seat.
Droplets are descending around us,
sparkling over the lake and
saffron-toasted trees.

In the corner of my eye, I see a couple like us,
Miss Sweepy Black Hair
and Miss Plaid Cardigan, Rolled Jeans.

A brown duck waddles-up to you,
you're good with animals
and there's something comforting
in the way you consume things slowly,
like I won't be left behind.

In the city book store,
we point at our representation
throughout the fantasy section.
It's always fantasy
and even in those, all but happy-endings.

"My personal library is better", I say,
and the date elongates.

You're intrigued by sun-bleached skulls
I have foraged and displayed.
I learn the one on my altar is in fact,
not a bird but a small rabbit.

Strung amber throbs around my bed
as we watch a sapphic film –
women's backs arching to the touch of their femme –
though, I fear to merely reach for your hand.

You borrow my books on the occult
and the art of taxidermy, but you've already
stuffed me
up – sabotaged my confidence.

First kiss

Turned on our sides,
shadows outline her smile
and deepen the beauty within her eyes.
Our noses are impossibly close.
I whisper a question to which, she nods –
take her jaw in my palm
and feel her mouth is that of clouds.
In between breaths, she laughs and I smile.
Says this answers a question she's had for a while.

We kiss again and my body reacts,
flipping her on her back.
My mind flinches at how quickly it was bypassed,
if for her, it was too fast.

Ripen Against Shadows

Shall we
ripen against shadows
as   thunder
before shaking   stalagmite limbs?
Make cathedrals of our karst caves
from sounds   loud enough
their echo   never wears out?
Shall you take the   hollowness of me
and bury   yourself in it
rebirth   us both
as crawling   creatures or
overhanging teachers
craving and giving nectar
over and
under again?

Crescendo

Crest.

Caressed.   Rest.

Her – I – Sea

Hips,
tongues;
the roll of waves,
one.
Wet, immersing and
surfing up my thighs.
Hands are tide,
under the full moon of her eyes.

I lower sink at the sight of
shadows – two resting crescents;
boats before a pink sun setting
or rising if I tip her by the hip –
rhythm causing days to flit.

Mounds draw to moans;
sweet kulning song, echoing through valley.
My fingers listen; herd.
Run, swoop, slither.
Every animalistic impulse in them, come hither.

My stifling lips, her soft fingertips
and breath in my ear.
It whispers over mountain peaks
shivers to sweat,
sweet temperature's temptress.
I, the harsh surface to her calm depths
but still the sea, aye the sea.

Siren and Sorceress

        Her heart,
         sealed
         within
         flasks;
        written
      and thrown
     though, never
   addressed to   shore.
   Waves crash   in-time
 with her pendu   lum. 'Tis
an ocean of truth   s unsung;
 spells and song   for fools
alike, but these   vice verses
neither can deny.   Courtship
   of scales and   satin –
   a passion so   powerful
   it transcends   the grave
    and raptu   res like
  ravens upon   their bones.
    More than   myths; is
this Siren to her Sorceress.

Savagefaction

Pulsating-sating. Sating.

Our Element

Reactive to my presence,
pulled to my touch. Caught in each other's orbit
as I puff from your pocket: stardust.

You illuminate as pressure builds,
lose and take form –
elevated in an electron/ic storm.

Overcome by the current,
we become something else.
Is this what it means

to be 'in your element'?
I fill you, feel you
transform with me. We are now, substance rare,

neither of us could be quite   as this,
by ourselves or with anyone else.
I can't leave

a single atom unturned or envious of another –
I worship every raised rhinestone of your skin,
see the shimmers of your every shiver.

Know there's transcendence in science,
confirmation in your constellations,
as I take you, layer by layer.

Shark

Inner wrists, a waterfall of veins,
my touch; a circling shark
never feeling so at home – in such an obscure place.

I examine the way her lashes flutter,
lips fall – parted – as she drowsily pushes into me.
I ache to bite her, drown her, drown myself in her,
until her breaths come short,
until they cut off altogether.

She utters things of silk and bone in a single tone.
I could never compose music – but I swear
the symphony of her cinching and softening   at my hand
is somewhere in Mozart's sphere.

Bodies mould together, mirror, before spilling
over like moody lakes upon summer stones.
Pin-prickled skin scintillating in trails
from where I've been
to where I've gone.

As we're sinking
and clenching each other into
a deepened stare.

Waves so roughly crash together yet whisk us away
into meditative states;
between her waterlines   everything stills.

9 Kisses of Medusa

1. From lips that (hiss) of steam and sparks you evoke in me
2. From lips that want nothing more than to (shed) you.
3. From lips seeking (heat) to treat cold-blood
4. From lips desiring to (devour) prey whole
5. From lips that (poison) and call it love-potion, symbolise (sin) and (sexuality) like they're the same thing
6. From lips that (constrict)
7. From lips (hibernating) to shut out the ice of your non-embrace
8. From lips of a creature (coiling) itself into a ring
9. From lips as (human) as can be

1.

So I slipped,
so you stuck me as Astrape,
e l e c t r i c i t y.
So nothing.

2.

You are no seductress
and say you were,
I am steadfast in my solitude.
I Refuse.
to lose my head again.

3.

Though, I'd never felt such desire,
to lick around abundant curves with my eyes.
To listen to rolling skin with my fingertips.
But I don't.

4.

I don't. There's a reason why 'romantic' entraps the word 'antic'.
Have you ever had Medusa kiss you with *all* that she can?
Stare at you with desire – direct – no doubt?
Her love; a curse to both you and herself.
I feel more or less like that.

5.

Of no divinity; how could I be, if I'm not even capable of tending to you with *all* of me?
How could I be, if I let my worth be dictated by this, something so mortal, so flawed?
You owe nothing to anyone.
Still, I ask – teach me or damn me
to worship you how you want to be.
How often, I bring you down to words when all I want is to lift you higher.
How may I do that from below you
– in any way but intimately? Tell me…

6.

How to stop turning such softness to stone
How to stop bringing you down to casing
How to stop speaking of other goddesses like they're any comparison.
I make the ethereal seem so small.
I ought to bite my tongue 'til it splits. Well, more than it is.
I ought to write you letters from that faraway place.
And I do.

7.

Anyone could fall
for you at first sight, but I mustn't meet your eyes.
You deserve someone who is sure and I only *fall*
short... so far short.

8.

Take my curse captive to your blessings.

9.

You say: love is blind,
people kiss with their eyes shut anyway,
I needn't send x's in metaphors anymore,
all these lips need be, is against yours.

Shark II

Have you ever seen a shark egg?
  If you have, you might understand
      the I tornado birth
    when you're around.
     Let me sweep my
    arms around you
  until swimming
 feels like
   flying.

Eclipsed

She whom dares defy the sun,
siphons the potency of witching hour
and steals the rarity of an eclipse
for her own eyes

spins my world into dusk.

A vision of triquetra,
the ways I wish to be tied to her.
Past, present, future.
Mind, body, spirit.

> Goddess gaze at me through third eye,
> complete this symbol with a final ring
> forged of storm and sky.
>
> Know, your chaos scares me not,
> I never gave a corsage
> nor even rose for the sun
> but what is in-between;
> the alignment of your being.
>
> Most sacred circle:
> circumference, of your finger.
> I purely wish to hold not possess
> and I know how you are turned against
> but in crescents you are blinding – no less.

To Wish for You

To wish for you
I must selfishly wish for many a thing.

I clutch charms, in hopes you've had the luck
to grow-up in a place where women like me, who love women like you
– aren't wrong, shunned or reprogrammed in 'love'.
That you were taught to explore instead of repress yourself.

I hush dandelions with secrets of you. Wistful they flee
into the folds of time with the intention of telling you.
I blush, though, still will their seeds to float down like snow
upon your mind; delicate moments of what could be.

I somersault silver coins over my shoulder
into fountains and wells. Knowing the water that polishes my wishes
is reused, reissued and my hopes subside in bottomless nightfall.
I summon to them, all men in your life, to be as such to you.
I know it to be cruel; though I never apologise
whilst on the same level as man.

In lucid dreams I rub golden lamps and tell the blue apparition
to travel into your sleep, plant orchids and farm oysters,
then examine your eyes for a spark of desire.
Perhaps, it provokes conversation beyond subconscious means;
who you are, what you want, your sexuality.
Things about yourself you may have never otherwise perceived.

When your birthday arrives, hell, I'd even blow out your candles;
steal your wish for mine if be told what exactly you were wishing for.
Do New Years resolutions overshadow
what you truly want with what you *should* want?

Maybe 'wish' was never the right word.
I'd never want to change you into something you aren't.
Though, I rather hoped that my desires weren't
out of reach
that I would know you at least well enough
to know who you are
or never could be – to me.

There is just one last romanticist's possibility,
that is:
you look up at night skies too,
desperately searching for that *glimmer and plummet*
or many
like the coin over my back,
like my heart in my chest.

And if I only had *one* wish
that needed no others – void of impulse –
it would be that you find yours,
in that sky.
Whatever it is.

With you content, at my side or otherwise,
I might understand why I yearn for you so much
or why I shouldn't.

Would you use that miracle on someone or something else?
Or would you use that request on me, to ask for you?
Have you already? Did the dandelions succeed?
Is this cycle, why we will never be?

Both too distracted beckoning our intrinsic synchronicity.

Seamless Incisions

The most seamless incisions are made by the sharpest blades.
You dither before my threshold.

Your smile stings
when it shines just as brightly upon every other person.

My voice breaks listening to yours
speak of him.

Your touch burns
knowing you only mean it as a friend.

Your pretty perfume rouses demons in my head
reminding me: I'm not the one you wore it for.

The taste of you is sweet I'm sure
– a sense you'll never gift me with, even unintentionally –
and my god, that is poison (the worst).

Can't you be dull?
Can't you be blunt with me, love?

Before we're in too deep,
let me hurt enough
to recoil.

War Paint

In a poppy-less field,
she lounges –
a lethal sort of serene.

You study her face, meticulously,
her brow does not crease

though light streaks down her face
like war paint –

Every contour an innocent captor.

Isn't she kind?
To care more about
your insides.

Love leaps over physicality,
but organs are not small trinkets.

"They're not valentine chocolates",
you repeat to the hollow of your chest.

Dear B,

There is a well of you inside me, built of teeth in place of stones.
Tell me how to dislodge my tongue
so I may tell you how it got that way to begin with,

how I can't meet your eyes
for much longer than a second
for fear I might fall – in a way you can see this time.

I'd tell you how those seconds make up a lifetime to me,
with the frequency I play them back.
We are strangers really,
I know that.

Aren't you aware of how you make my heart rupture
with the speed its own beats?
Do you not feel how the world shakes
and blurs
around us, when our eyes meet?

I don't even have the capacity
to be self-conscious around you.
You fill me to my brim,
words overflow out my mouth
from disarrayed thought patterns.

Do you know how long my fingers have been
tapping over blue light
– searching in thirst, for any radiance of you –
craving to be surveying your skin instead?

Scouring your bios, your biomes, for rainbows:
you're quite clearly *pot* of gold,
but I can't touch unless I know.

It'd be so easy to breathe you in, get higher than I've ever been.
Don't you know that's
why my stomach tightens; fear my head might lighten
when your smile sparks.

I wouldn't be surprised if the secrets of the sun were written in it;
the way it brightens my own face and I can't turn down the dial. God,
I adore you in light-years, you know.

I've gone back, breathed out, into my cloudy home but still, you warm me.

I'll never be able to tell you any of this anyway;
for these words to hold truth
my tongue must stay glued –
if it isn't, maybe these words aren't worth saying.
They lose credibility and meaning
and darling, there is nothing meaningless
about the effects of you.

Honey

You must have suffused
the softest feathers into your cheeks,
spat-out every stone
to be gifted these lips of peach.

I scry for answers you will give
only unto his lips.

B – Be – Bee;
why must your name be
a letter containing all of the words
I've not been taught
nevertheless, feel
more than he can say.
A question, an urge,
a sight
like how 'buzz' is both
a sound and a feeling?

B, Honey, you're a taste and a colour.

A progression with every pronunciation,
like the pulsing timer in my chest.

Thicker than the blood
I chose you over,
and now I'm sticky
and stuck.

The Beast

Selfish, I thought all human actions –
be it, in one way or another;
subconsciously, deliberately.
Even to love someone.
That was, until I met you.
You, the one whom did not love me back
and indicated no chance of it.

I know,
a heart is only as broken as it is focused;
how pain is a reaction,
but also, something we react *out* of.
So why couldn't I?

I strain to fathom a benefit from my troubles.

Was putting my loyalty on a pedestal,
the fastest way to take you off of it in-turn?

Do we only fall for the unattainable
because they seem untaintable?

If self-interest drives every desire;
was your impossibility simply, an outlier I reached for
to prove to myself I wasn't the user
we all are?

To put it simply,
if we were beauty and the beast,
it would be you *not* loving me
that made me less savage.

Why Do You Go to a Man?

I want to ask if you're happy with him
but I already know you are.

and then I wonder if I'm hooked on self-harm.

Is he beautiful?
Does he help you brush your hair?
Can he dance? Hold your legs while you handstand?

It's said, you're supposed to be happy in yourself
before you can be happy with someone else –
and what's of you, is of other women too.

So why do you go to a man?

If he can't tell you first-hand, he understands?
If his hands will never know you like they know himself?
If he won't always have a tampon or hairband in his purse?

You go to a man because that's how you are,
I'm acting like I don't know,
I'm acting like it makes you any less.

You go to a man the same way
I *want* to go to you.
There's nothing wrong with either,
only my misfortune.

Cryptologist

I loved with reason
because you are all the reasons there are to love.

There-in lies the issue,
my heart cracked the same way,

like a code
I was convinced I needed to (further) break.

I connected dots, followed morse-als back,

just to understand
where you discerned I lacked.

Never You

You were never just a heartbreak.
You were a thousand reopening wounds.
Every woman, I so much as walked past,
after us
     broke my heart
          with the simple fact:

               she could never be you.

Encyclopedia of Botanic Symbology

When I tie off this final
bouquet, I hope you see the
messages I've left
of pollen and vein.

See the **moonflower** means,
dreaming of love and that's our
beginning. But they only bloom
at night and don't survive long
– so take them in quickly
and imagine they're not lethal.

When I first saw you, *I fell
instantly*, I think that's what
lavender coloured roses mean.
But it was **red daisies** I wanted
to nestle into your hair. Which
is to say, *"you are beautiful but
unaware"*.

I whispered "give me *strength*,
oak leaves" each time you
passed me by. Knowing my
mouth agape, speaks louder
than any words I could take-
back or deny.

You told me *my thoughts follow
you into your dreams*. I blamed
the **white egret orchid** for its
deceit.

But your arms *welcome*d me
like **wisterias**. And **rainflowers**
grew in the whites of your eyes;
dizzying stars
as you claimed to *love me –
likewise*.

I would include the **acacia**, but
it doesn't seem fitting. We were
a *secret union*, yes… but it
didn't look that cheerful.
It was more like **blackthorn**,
hope against adversity.

Yes, your **Queen of the Night**,
such the cynic. *"Enjoy small
moments because they do not
last"*. I did, long after zephyr
sentiments had orbited and
passed.

I swallowed the **Mallow**:
consumed by love. And the
Mulberry to follow it up. It
grows in the garden of my
childhood home, weeping and
alone. It means, *'I will not
survive you'* when given to a
love. Isn't that the most
painfully beautiful meaning out
of all the above?

So have the **cranberry**, *the
cure for heartache*. Take **pink
carnations** and know *I'll never
forget you*. The **spindle tree**
says "your image is engraved
on my heart" and finally…

"take care" I use **azaleas**, to
sign off.

Hoping that even if you can't
remember the individual
symbols. You'll still see our
story here; simply from the
beauty. Remember how we
grew each other. The gratitude.
The regard. Flowers as a whole,
signify… us, fleeting and
susceptible to frost.

In Memory of Marie
M.J.W. (28 January 2000 - 6 September 2021)

You wrote poetry without realising it;
prophecies of your own perishing.
As if – somewhere deep within you – you knew.

The day before your accident:
'Death always haunts me.'
'What if I lose you?'

and the day you left, your last words:
'…coming out of my first relationship to
See you on the other side'

Ever reliable, you kept promises after death.
Singing, 'Dreams, that's where I have to go
to see your beautiful…'
and indeed, you met me there.
but for you,

'I don't want to fly over to attend your funeral'
those were your words, inherited by my mouth,
because I never knew of yours until it had passed.

I grieved you as a friend and no more,
ashamed of emotion if not behind closed doors.

Your mother reached out,
said you spoke highly of me,
I thought of my own family, the guilt
of not telling them a thing.

I am not as burdened as the mother
who lost her child,
and I will not be another burden to a mother
who has lost her child.

Though, I can't stop thinking about how I pushed you down and away.
You never ran out of forgiveness
all the times I never asked
like a mother,
my own mother I never gave the benefit of the doubt.

My Blood

For my cousin, Jacynta

With wisdom, you brush my cheek –
guardian and guide of mine
though you may not admit.

You've made,
this weight upon your shoulders
but wings –
ascended ashes of a more
abrasive society
you've lived.

I admire you – my blood –
one who heals
instead of causing more there-of.

You are deep, strong, resilient;
like unbroken rivers.

And as simple as it is to say,
it's also great, having girl talk
that is actually *girl* talk.

Dating Apps and Country Towns

Straight men who believe
more consistency will cure
the gay girl in you.

Threesomes; more reasons
to drink and prune the garden
with ever **blunt** teeth.

And your high, high school
bitch building evidence to
out you to your friends.

*'Sorry, there's no one
new in your area',* Oh.
Oh. Thank god for that!

If It's Physical
Letter to the Male Gaze

It's how earrings brush their neck.
The way their jeans crease when they tread.
The shadows of their shoulder blades.
An eyebrow slightly raised.
It's the build of their backs
or the front of their thighs.
The lines on their chins when they smile.
Sorbet jawlines.
It's stomachs like neatly folded laundry
or ribs resembling inverted wings, peaking from their chests.
It's their hair tumbling out, mess of unrest.
There are so many more remarkable sights I could list
other than breasts.

Rum and Vanilla Extract
For A.E.T.

I still don't understand why I can't let you go,
I miss you almost every day,
tell strangers stories of you
that happened five years ago,
think about the way we used to wear each other's clothes,
lie in the same bed and talk 'til 2am.
How we'd spin across your lounge room floor,
argue over which dance moves should come next.

Sometimes I ask myself if I loved you.
Romantically, I don't think I did
but **I know** I loved you.
Intensely.
I feel, that's something in its own regard.

I wonder if you think of me. I know you mustn't.
You've changed, been sucked into the fast city,
where little people like me don't fit in,
aren't worth considering.
You don't look back and I'm glad; you're such an empowered woman now.
But also distraught.
How you could forget about me?
The girl who held you when you were small and breaking.
Is there any part of her still within you somewhere?
I don't know whether to hope there is
or isn't.

If she's not there anymore, where is she?
Where's that girl,
who would write me letters longer than my bad nights lasted?
who cared enough to read 22 pages of cringey middle school lyrics?
who would be swallowed up by a bush just to pick me the brightest daisy?
Maybe she fell into another, never to re-emerge.

Tell me, over all these years, I never knew the real you?
I swear I *knew* the real you
but last time we spoke you lied. Didn't give me a second of your time.
Trod on my heart like we had no history, as if there wasn't a time where you meant everything to me.

I can't know what I really want, when all I want
is what we had back then –
I'm almost sure that in this day, at our age, that doesn't exist.
We haven't spoken in a year but I still can't leave you in the past.
Tell me how you let go of all we had?

I miss your mum and your psycho cat.
I miss the way your hair would frizz in the mornings
and the liquor we choked on at my house.
I muted you on all of my media feeds, but not for the reason you would think.
It hurts to see your smiling face and the girl beside you...
I was so easy to replace.

I know I'm being selfish, I'm not trying to hold you back
but sometimes I wish you would message
to say you were sorry
for how things ended up,
that you would do anything to have me back.

You know, for you, I would do the same
but I'm over being a second choice.
You preyed on my empathy,
I don't trust to give you that side of me now.
I bet you don't even know what you did or
when I finally snapped.
It wasn't just the end of a year but the end of me
always 'being there'.

How could I want something that will always been tarnished?
Why do memories of you burn like rum but read as vanilla extract?
How could a loss of a friendship destroy me more than any of my breakups?

Was it because we never fought, never allowing me to call you out
and close that door?
I miss you but I'm too proud to say it.
How is it relevant now anyway?
So I'll pretend that maybe I don't miss you.

Perhaps, I just miss simpler times,
or a good reason to drink alcohol from medicine cups.
I could miss hearing some bad taste in music, once in a while.
I could miss fully clothed jetty jumps.

I could miss being attacked by your feline (carmine dotted-lines; always a better reason to cry).
I could miss all of this garbage,
Couldn't I?

Extended

This is the second poem I've written to you,
I imagine where the first is, on the back of that photo album, a promise, a gift.
Now, an accidental form of sym(pathetic) magick,
likely shoved in a corner collecting dust
because neither do I, remember what it was.
Like that Valentines card, you thought you'd lost or tossed.
When really, another girl found it discarded on the locker room floor
and thought I deserved
my own words more.

Elsa

You messaged me today. First time in years.
Now that I've pulled your knife out
from between my ribs,
I almost wish you'd aimed better.
Hit the part of my heart that holds our memories.
If I had to bleed something, why couldn't it have been those?
They call me the Ice Queen –
but never checked your middle name.

Bloody Mary
Mary Worth

"Bloody Mary" I whispered thirteen times
as she ignited me with her flames,
had me spinning dizzily in the dark.
It started with a candlelit date, she's never left since.
I don't mind this curse; might she haunt me forever
and I would burn with her.
I see a promise; spellbinding commitment.

She understands how to honour a hooded woman,
as a cloaked witch herself,
shows me what it is, to have a silver bullet,
shot between my hips.

***

Over time, I see, perhaps, I only sought
self-communion with my darker half.
Seeing my womanly form, my frame;
hung seditiously in someone else.

There's a fine line; a fine glass,
between
bringing out the beauty already existent in the umbratical,
and romanticising a predator because her shadow reflects my own.
So frequently, I get the two confused.

I wasn't spinning, I was turning for her.
I wasn't blinded by beauty; she'd gouged out my eyes.
Now I'm trapped behind something so fragile.

Never confuse one's identity with psychology
or view your soul externally.
All portrayed in the reflector is a lie
taken from your insides and wagered against you.
The blood upon Mary's exterior; such horror
even having emanated from a
healthy heart.

On-stage Chemistry

They ricochet off each other's auras,
sewing each other into being
with every   sin—   u o   u   s   arch of their backs
and lull of their heads.

Did you ever see such a duet?
So fervent and saccharine.
The slipping embraces and curling of toes.
Oxytocin essence lingering in the air between their skin.

Phantom colours that span on through the dark, past any spotlight;
space they've long spiralled out of.

Crystal Shop Date
D.C. – Journey Entry 28/10/2021

My boots lick the grey off Rundle
towards the flower shop.
I sweep up a purple bouquet
and ask the shop assistant if I look okay,

"...it's my first date with them – with *a them.*"
It's also my first coming-out to a stranger
and her warmth takes off the price tag –
my arms are stemming again.

Walking towards the kissing silver orbs,
bluebells spilling over brown paper,
when I first catch the azure of their eyes
and earthy attire.

The bus doors flip open
and we plan our next outing
before arrival at the initial.

Where crystal points like configured castles;
whisper of times passed.
An immersion of drapings and geodes
from the chiming door, to the back.

I acquire a stone the colour of their hair; apatite
in hands, but our stomachs we humour.

In a café, they twist a straw
from chocolate-adorned glass.
Nervously blush and laugh.

As we part,
wings of fae wave from their lobes,
a Clairo song flutters across my mind
and follows me home.

Extended

> I should have known when I invested
> in the garnet – devotion, commitment –
> and they chose apache tears.

Phantom

Their phantom underpinned
by October's reminiscence.
As subtle as a shadow on the wall
as jarring as where it could have come from
or in this instance, what didn't come of it.

Two Life Paths

1.

I was
 seeking
  someone
  to have
  fun with
   but when
    we met,
         love;
       until
      I met
     her
    fear
    -lessness.
    Later,
    I
     grew
      jealous

          I told
         myself
        not to
       look back
      but never
       fully
       left *her*
        in the past
       as I
       continued
on my path.

2.

              So much
               of my
                life
               spent
              alone.
             I was
           scared of
          gave
          me
          safety
          and
          depth.
          Except, I
          couldn't
          do the
         inner work.

         I
         realised
          my
         mistake first –
        apologised
         but it was
              too
               late.

Crimes You Want Me to Commit

Tell me something,
do I make you feel afraid?
Come on – say it
to my face.

Clever woman, what are these games?
Is intimate dating
too intimidating
for your taste?

You say you want trust,
but do you know
how to form it
without a little dangerous?

I could show you
with the softest touch
but you're set on tough love.

Go on, lock me up
when *you're* in need of release.
I will fill your every cell
with crimes you want me to commit.

The Whole Damn Arsenal

                    Who
                    needs
                    cupid,
                when she's
                 the whole
                damn arsenal?
                 She pulls
                with the bow
                 of her lips,
               lacerates with
         the blades of her shoulders,
                   brings
                   men to
                    their
                    knees
                   in tank
                    -tops,

   takes shots rapid-fire,
 from a glass or her Can*n*on SLR.
 Becoming the art in artillery.
 Such a high
 calibre
 woman
 but I…

                        I am
                         content
                           as simply,
                            the archer
                          of her
                        spine.

My Crypt/tonight

It's sensuously scarring. –

    the way you dance more in-time with me
    than my own shadow.

        Maroon, now less a colour
        than a dare; my fate you fashion for me –

Hands knit like knives,
your revival I may never survive;

        sharp inhalations
        a sweet annihilation

            on this night so full, we find ourselves
            ticking over to the 25th hour.

Assassin
J.S., A.Y., G.N., T.V. & D.C.

Once, there was a lifeguard who wrote me 100 letters.
My name on each envelope handwritten in experimental fonts,
red roses woven through calligraphy.

After that, there was a carpenter,
who handcrafted me bookshelves
and a photo frame from the finest redwood.

There was a poet who wrote me
the most amorous verses

and a musician who couldn't get me off his mind,
so wrote a song which stuck in mine.

There was even an artist who drew me, unknowingly.
Spinning in a green gown, open-backed with a satin opulence.

In each letter, I was a different word for fateful.
In the picture frame, I had my arms around his neck.
In the poem, I was her 'impenetrable fortress'.
In the song, a 'cynical' confliction.
In the artwork, I was titled 'assassin'.

This is all to say,
I've become poetry, a song, a masterpiece –
but all I've ever wanted is

                                        to be someone's final girl.

Observations of Floristry Student
Notes on Decomposition

Rose

As she dies, her body goes soft;
I unfurl and rub the inner buttery folds.
Rigor mortis is late this season.

After the water dissipates, she will stiffen.
In a year, flake and break away from herself.
I collect her pieces which spoke to me
and burn them.

Her ash is momentary warmth.

Observations of Floristry Student
Notes on Decomposition

Lily; 'I Dare You to Love Me'

Is it corrupt? To have noticed she was something of a daydream?
Amiable eyes, wonderous blush,
the coven of her arms.

I'm afraid of what it means to 'want'.
Afraid to become an ulterior motive,
Afraid to be known.
Flaws announced with each closer examination.

Is my kindness ever genuine, if I notice?
If I write this?

Is this why I find myself eternally alone?
My essentialism, to have only what I 'need'
I once thought protected and kept me free.
Now, I reflect on those relationships,
their sense of urgency;
trauma bonds, co-dependency.

Then, I cannot help to think, it's better this way:
to be an uncomplicated stranger,
never to see a decomposition.

This is how I outlive myself;
the temporary type of beautiful I am.

Last Words

She wanted to hold my hand
through the scary parts of the movie,
I let her possess me.

She threaded her fingers softly through my hair,
"I can give you braids".
I let her cross me.

Springy curls framing naked eyes
I watched her undress.
I let her undo me.

Shutter clicks, said her camera
was meant to capture the complex
I let her shoot me.

Once she called me 'a knock-out'.
If I had a chance,
it would've been then.

The Morgue

"BODY OF UNIDENTIFIED WOMAN FOUND IN ADELAIDE MORGUE"

I had opened to her completely. My mind, eyes & heart stretched,
arms and lips gaped to receive her and having cleared enough space
in me, to place her emptiness, she fled. Hourglass of antigravity sand –
leaving me at the bottom while taking all that I had.
She, not a grain, but a husk; I repetitively reached for through
rewound time. rewound time. re-(*wound*) time.
I thought I'd broken for her *then*…though I see now,
a cavern in my skull, tear in my chest, terror yawned eyes.
In these fragments of before, I relearn
the relief of being an illusion
to myself; owning this
dissection in every
aspect.
My bones, organs
and muscles – all
finally, taste the bite of
fresh air, so alive as   l u n g s
if not anything else; if not themselves.
Becoming a past-life before death. Openness
that begs to feel good again. The way it should have been
if she'd known value in *mutual* scavenging. Question
the cause before deciding on an affect. Anyone working on a body
knows to sew it up, not leave it to rot. Thus, the reason I am here,
waiting on an autopsy table. On this metallic bed, I may finally know
rest.

"Autopsy revealed mutilation to the body was inflicted ante-mortem. Cause of death suspicious. *Inside*-job suspected. Case left *open*".

Catacombs
For G.M.N.

Give me the kiss of death
in the catacombs of France,
frisk me in old gaols,
howl my   name through   ghost towns.
Hold me down,
then   teach me how to   escape
but never   let me go.
Let's make the neighbour's ears bleed
as we sing off-key.
These are her words my mind repeats.
She   wants   me
the way I want her;
respectfully *recklessly*.

Immortality

For G.M.N.

I dare not say her name only
carcasses of words.

Tiller of the soil; she could be the one
who unspools my lines with a glance
unperplexed; unlike anyone else.
Would I care? Or would I thank her?

Most know more than they speak,
if that's so, how intelligent must she be?

She says you find your *humanness* in poetry;
and it's funny
because there, and also in a person like her,
I'll find immortality as well.

Afterlife

You are a type of beautiful deserving of your own words.

I would re-discover and decipher every lost language
just to call you beautiful in a different way, every *coupled* day.

        I would catch every raindrop falling – at this moment – to earth,
            just so your tears would have the company they deserve.

I would master the art of telepathy
just so you may take refuge in your mind while your hand's not in mine.

                      Even travel back in time
     just to rewrite scriptures people misuse against you and our kind.

Darling, I would die and go to the afterlife
just to inform the gods: they must bow before you, as you arrive.

           For you, this could never be enough but I would do it all
                just to give you a small definition of my love.

She to Her

She, to her body had surrendered...

I'm tantalised with the notion ancient scriptures
could be encrypted with forbidden romance.
Lovers, taking 'She' and 'Her' as their own names;

the closest the closeted, or any lover,
could ever come together.
Morphing seamlessly into one,
since not accepted as a couple.

Forgotten but spoken of
every day over millennia,
even through the mouths
of those who wished to close theirs.
if they had known…

and later, / when her shivers set in / and she was drenched in sweat, / she could only think of how / her breath was taken / and she was the one responsible / for her undoing. / God, the praying she was compelled to do; head low / with her knees bent as / she held / up her hands. /

Fractural Femme Fatale Lyrics

Madam X,

"Have we met before?"
I got kinda drunk
memories are slipping –
your name an echo in the dark.

What are the chances
there's no other?

What will it take?
'til it's just us two
and the distant moon.

I want to
have more than blind faith;
decipher your demeanour –
curl up
in the   parts of you   that
won't heal.

          I like the way your mouth
          moves,

          from every point of view.

          lipstick – blood-red

          breath magnified

                    in bloom –
          smoke
          a crutch;
          you know it's never enough.

          Take off
          all you
                painted white,
          Give me
          your polluted marrow,
          nothing left to hide.

          Are you listening?

I want your
trembling
hand grenade
        ex p l o s i on
thunderous,
caught in a rush
erosion.

                                      I want your born-again
                                      shadows
                                      that spill over.

                                      I want
                                                  your salt
                                                              sedation,
                                      your

                                                  soft disposition
                                    turned
                                                monsoon.

                                      Make a mess.
                                                                 Misbehave

                                      Michelle. Michelle.
                                      I'm mad for you
                                      and the distant moon.

Future Me This

The heart and life lines of my palms
have always been broken up,
chained and splintering out like branches.

Once, my ex's sister – holding a palmistry book,
told me this means I'm a cheater.
And if I'm honest, she's not wrong:

I was enamoured with someone else while I was with him,
not so much an individual as part I wouldn't need to play.

So, I split the deck myself.

Practised how to predict   and I could summon
just about anything except

there was never that sign, for my someone to arrive.
Never that card, for my someone to sign.

But I'm still thinking about
muddy boots at the door,
logs lining our walls,
fire crackling and sticks snapping.
I'm still thinking about someone who'll count birds with me,
listen to their warbling.
Palms pressing the soles of my feet
to wake me in the morning.
My mugs of green tea leaving rings
next to their choice of hot drink.
I'm still thinking literature and lavender.
Snow and sage.
How I want to trek, pitch tents,
strike matches just for the scent.

Distant love, I will keep shuffling those cards
with my crooked hands
until they're crushing peppercorn under your nose,
sassafras, geraldton wax
and sure, the occasional rose.

I crave a tenderness to believe in,
needless of talismans;
a place more protected by openness than walls.

So future me this,
we wake slow and read old letters.
The overcast, drizzly weather,
all we know of the outside world before 10:47.

We make breakfast,
lemon and strawberry sinking into the scars
of chopping boards.
Chopping boards, that know nothing of fault-lines.

I write you oddly specific poems

>   like about the moment you throw a shirt over her head
>   and your hair is tucked into the collar... or scruffed up if it's
>   shorter.
>
>   All the ways I want to be a passenger
>   to your passages – becoming these passages.

And sure, you'll tell me these are the most ridiculous words
to exist.
Tell me they suck!
Test me in all the ways you want.

But one day...
you'll refuse to give the poem back
or let me change it.
I'll call this a win.

Later, I'll pull you in,
we'll slow dance –
backlit by the amber glow of the oven.
'Cigarettes After Sex' playing on imaginary vinyl.

Love, if there's a need to fear
it will be in the shallows, not depths
of breaths.

If there's a need for *space*
nebulas will form across my eyes

before any judgement.

This is also to say, I will write poems to someone I cannot see;
have not met yet.
So when I do, there's proof I can miss them better than anyone else;
Time travel may be the finest gift I can give
and the best reason for the time-lines of my hands
to be split.

Hearth

If our passion burns us out,
I will have you know:
your chest landmarks my home

– because it's always the (heart)h
which remains; standing amongst fallen stones –

and if there's this,
the fire within us
never truly kills
nor dies at all.

Thank you for reading!

For all business-related enquiries please email:
slade.enquiries@gmail.com

Notes

While everything I wish to express is embedded within the poems already. There are a few exceptions where I make reference to science, history, folklore and such. These may not be as obvious to identify to readers who haven't studied the subjects. I include a quick overview of some of the poem's references below.

Crime Scene

The poem as a whole, is a remark on the criminalisation of homosexuality throughout history. Moreover, how strong women are notorious for making the best out of dire situations. The imagery of the red string serves as three symbolic references. Firstly, the red-string is perceived on the pinboard of an unsolved case. Secondly, it morphs into the lasers of guns. Most importantly, the red string is a nod to a Chinese Legend which describes an invisible red thread tied to our pinkie fingers. This string is said to link us to people we will make history with. These are the people we are joined to by fate, regardless of circumstances, time or distance.

Our Element

References to basic science: covalent bonding of elements. As well as, what makes stars twinkle (starlight passing through layers of earth's atmosphere).

Rum and Vanilla Extract

I include this poem in this collection because it's the most real, unfiltered thing I've written about loving another woman, even in a platonic way. I wanted to share a different take on having to hide your feelings for someone. How even in this aromatic and asexual relationship dynamic, you can still have feelings for someone that are larger than socially acceptable.

Bloody Mary

There are many variations of the legend of Bloody Mary and I'll briefly explain two. The first being the most popular story and the second, the one explored in this poem.
Some believe Bloody Mary to be the Queen of England in 1553-1558, who killed around 300 people by burning them at the stake for not converting to Catholicism. The name, 'Bloody Mary' a reference to how much blood she had on her hands after killing all of these people.

According to another legend, Bloody Mary was a woman called Mary Worth, who was perceived as a witch in her town. She was rumoured to bathe in children's blood to stay young, which is probably where the name comes from (in this version). In the end, she was shot in the hip with a silver bullet by a farmer and then tied to a stake to burn to death. Before she died, she cursed anyone who dared say her name (three or 13 times) before a mirror – saying that it would summon her ghost, who'd steal their soul for her own, burn it like the villagers burnt her at the stake and then trap them behind the mirror with her for all eternity.

War Paint

Is about a common sapphic experience of not being able to differentiate feelings of envy to attraction. Most often related to by younger people who have repressed their sexuality and overcommit to partners quickly due to low self-esteem.

Elsa

The friend this is for, did come back into my life post writing this. We reconnected after she read some of my poetry I posted online and we resolved our problems. We have moved past our conflict and are both grateful to still have each other, in our lives.

Two Life Paths

This poem can be read by following the two lines, representing the life paths of two women as they meet. One line is defined in italics for ease of reading. At the end, the lines part but weave back towards each other at different levels. This represents the two characters looking back at their relationship at different times.

On-Stage Chemistry

Inspired by the first time I saw a dance performed by two women as partners.

Fractural Femme Fatale Lyrics

This poem is comprised song lyrics either by sapphic music artists or songs with a femme fatale feel to them. The line-breaks separate different lyrics. To give the poem a touch of my own, I selected one

word being 'erosion'. Ultimately, this is an excuse to give you a playlist of bangin' songs. See the songs referenced as follows:
'Madam X' by Allie X, 'Spiracle' by Flower Face, 'When You Say My Name' by Chandelier Leighton, 'Michelle' by Sir Chloe, 'Explosion' by Zolita, 'She's My Religion' by Pale Waves, 'Criminal' by Issadora Ava, 'Do You' by Morganne, 'More Than a Friend' by girli.

Acknowledgements

I would like to thank *Beyond Queer Words* for publishing 'She's the Skeleton in my Closet' in the February 2023 Edition of their Anthology. Also thank you to *Australian Poetry Journal* where 'Spiralled Shell' first appeared in the *divergence, relevance* 12.1.

A massive thank you to my uncle, Tim Slade, author of 'The Walnut Tree', for always making time for my poetry. Thank you for dissecting every word (of every version) of this book, enduring long phone calls to assist me in editing, alerting me to poetry competitions amongst many, many other generosities.

I am ever grateful to my mum for putting through the Davis Dyslexia Program, without your perseverance, I would never have discovered the beauty of literature. In all-seriousness, I would still be avoiding books and writing. You are responsible for countless opportunities in my life.

Thank you to my dad for always being supportive, open-minded and ready to adapt to anything I throw at him. You are my biggest mentor, advocate and friend.

Thank you to my sister, Claire for encouraging me to get out of my comfort zone and go to poetry readings. For being a sounding board and reliably blunt without making me feel judged. (I   promise   I   will   read   slower.)

Thank you Jacynta, for always being a safe place. Sharing your own poems and experiences with me.

Thank you to any other friends who've helped me edit my poems. Specifically, Analeisha for her ongoing support and affirmations. Thank you for allowing me to include some pretty brutal poems about you in this collection. I'm so grateful we have rebuilt our friendship now.

Finally, I'm thankful for the poetry community I've found at Adelaide's open mics. Specifically, Mixed Bag Poetry organised by Cecelia. There, I have met the most open-hearted people.

Spider Silk Art Series

A collection of poetic art prints featuring romantic moments between sapphic couples, interweaving short lines from the book 'Spider Silk'. From starry scenes to garden house intimacy, these prints make thoughtful gifts, paired with poetry plus your choice of flowers and chocolates.

All artworks are original by author, Danah Slade. Available for a limited time from her website and Esty shop.

Books - Get the Set

No Promises

Slade's debut poetry book *'No Promises'* spans over eight years, sharing the story of a dyslexic falling in love with language and providing insight into how our relationships shape us. The collection serves as a companion for those navigating emotional turmoil and taking accountability for their healing.

Vertebrae Letters

A collection of poetry highlighting the importance of being attuned to our bodies and the environments around us. The author channels poetry from her lived experience with clinical depression, endometriosis, chronic fatigue, anxiety, derealisation and so on. From dark to light, poems of ill health transform into words of healing. Inspired by the crystallised sap on trees and scenes of rain cascading down steps, *Slade* illustrates the transcendental effects of observing nature and what it means to find hope in the smallest moments.

Spider Silk

The very book you have in your hands now! Why don't you tell us what this book meant to you on Goodreads (: all feedback is deeply appreciated.

About the Author

At the age of 22, Danah Slade published her debut poetry collection, 'No Promises', as an inspiration to other dyslexic writers and individuals healing from loss. Her poems have appeared in publications such as the 'Australian Poetry Journal', 'Beyond Queer Words Anthology' and 'StylusLit'. Currently, she resides in Adelaide, South Australia pursuing the art of fire spinning.

IG: @thepoisonouspoetess
@danahslade

www.ingramcontent.com/pod-product-compliance
Lightning Source LLC
Chambersburg PA
CBHW020543080526
44583CB00013B/965